# GENERAL GRANT BY MATTHEW ARNOLD

WITH

A Rejoinder by Mark Twain

# GENERAL GRANT

BY

## MATTHEW ARNOLD

WITH

## A Rejoinder by Mark Twain

---

*Edited with an Introduction*

BY

JOHN Y. SIMON

---

THE KENT STATE UNIVERSITY PRESS

*Kent, Ohio, & London, England*

03  02  01  00  99  98  97  96  95      5  4  3  2  1

*Library of Congress Cataloging-in-Publication Data*
Arnold, Matthew, 1822–1888.
General Grant / by Matthew Arnold ; with a rejoinder by Mark Twain ;
edited and with an introduction by John Y. Simon.—[2nd ed.]
p.    cm.
ISBN 0-87338-524-1 (alk. paper)
1. Grant, Ulysses S. (Ulysses Simpson), 1822–1885.  Memoirs.
2. Grant, Ulysses S. (Ulysses Simpson), 1822–1885.
3. Presidents—United States—Biography.
4. Generals—United States—Biography.
5. United States. Army—Biography.
6. Twain, Mark, 1835–1910—Political and social views.
I. Simon, John Y.  II. Title.
E672.A3A76   1995
973.8'2'092—dc20
[B]              94-36413

British Library Cataloging-in-Publication Data are available.

# C O N T E N T S

———

# Preface to the Second Edition

Publication twenty-eight years ago of Matthew Arnold's notable essay on Ulysses S. Grant's *Memoirs*, accompanied by Mark Twain's rejoinder, represented an attempt by the Ulysses S. Grant Association to announce and publicize its project of preparing a comprehensive edition of everything written by Grant. Soon after organization of the Grant Association in 1962, I had developed a plan to publish these documents in fifteen volumes. I have long since forgotten how I arrived at that number, which was probably influenced by the statement in the *Dictionary of American Biography* that Grant wrote "as little as possible" and by William B. Hesseltine's complaint about "the almost complete lack of Grant manuscripts." Unfortunately, we disseminated the fifteen-volume figure so widely that it returns to haunt us after the publication of twenty plump volumes of *The Papers of Ulysses S. Grant* has only carried the correspondence into the second year of the Grant presidency.

Grant was a prolific writer, one who rarely wrote at length but wrote often. He maintained friendships, conducted business, waged war, and administered the government all through handwritten communications. The Grant correspondence proved rewarding because Grant played a crucial role in momentous historical events both as general and president. Beyond that, he was so much a man of his time, representing both strengths and weaknesses of the American character, that to understand him was a step toward understanding millions of his countrymen. Simultaneously, Grant was unique and even mysterious. After leaving the White House he stated that he had never entered the army except with regret and had never left it except with pleasure. As for the presidency, he had "never quite forgiven" himself for agreeing to serve. This unmilitary general and reluctant president continues to fascinate.

Only poverty drove him to write his memoirs, yet he had always been an able writer. During the Civil War, he insisted on drafting his own reports, allowing staff officers merely to insert dates, figures, and relevant documents. Even on the battlefield Grant did not dictate messages but wrote them himself. Early in the war he sometimes drafted orders for his adjutant to sign. Grant's confidence in his writing ability reflected the same self-assurance displayed in his generalship.

Grant's Civil War correspondence is direct and precise, unemotional and unostentatious. Few letters involved advance preparation, first drafts, or secretarial assistance. Most express thoughts as they came to mind. Crossed-out words or sentences indicate a shift of thought or emphasis. Grant composed as many as thirty-five orders in a single day. He frequently wrote while conferring with commanders, surrounded by chattering staff officers, or while shells exploded nearby. Sentences were clear even when circumstances were complex, and recipients knew exactly what Grant expected. He reduced complex issues to fundamentals and struck through the fog of circumstance.

Grant's mastery of language appeared in his February 16, 1862, letter to Confederate general Simon B. Buckner, commanding Fort Donelson. "Yours of this date proposing Armistice, and appointment of commissioners, to settle terms of capitulation is just received. No terms except an unconditional and immediate surrender can be accepted. I propose to move immediately upon your works." Grant covered the entire subject in three sentences, the first merely restating the substance of the letter he had received. The second sentence, dependent upon Buckner's willingness to surrender, continues in the passive voice. The final sentence shifts to the active voice to eliminate any doubt that Grant intended "to move immediately upon your works." The word "propose" appears in both the first and third sentences—in the first to restate Buckner's intentions, in the third to declare those of Grant. That word recurred in Grant's letter of May 11, 1864, from Spotsylvania to Secretary of War Edwin M. Stanton: "I propose to fight it out on this line if it takes all summer." Half an hour later Grant repeated the phrase, which he recognized as entirely appropriate, in a letter to General Henry W. Halleck, now in the form of "propose to fight it out on this line if it takes me all Summer." On reflection, he crossed out "me," a word that added nothing to the sentence and actually diminished its impact by focusing attention on the dogged determination of the commander while ignoring that of his troops.

"Propose" made a late dramatic reappearance in Grant's preface to his *Memoirs,* which he opened with the quoted motto "Man proposes and God disposes." Surveying his remarkable career from Mount McGregor, Grant echoed the bewilderment of contemporaries called upon to appraise the triumphs and tragedies of this undemonstrative man. General William T. Sherman concluded that Grant was a mystery to himself as well as to others.

Early in the war, Grant wrote that he could not find enough loyal men in southeast Missouri "to save Sodom." Learning that Generals Samuel R. Curtis and William S. Rosecrans were "calling for more troops" to defend Missouri, Grant responded that "you would hear the same call if they were stationed in Maine." In exasperation, Grant wrote that "Rosecrans should be removed and some one else placed in command. It makes but little difference who you assign it would be an improvement." Even in official correspondence Grant used language playfully and inventively. His specialty, however, was understatement.

The simplicity found in Grant's prose appeared elsewhere in his life. Grant's silence before he announced his military decisions bewildered staff officers who could not follow his thought processes; as Henry Adams quipped, "they were not sure that he did think." Words flowing onto paper in hundreds of field dispatches contradict that gibe, as does Grant's rapid adjustment to changing conditions in the May 1863 encirclement of Vicksburg and the lightning strokes of the Appomattox campaign.

Meeting Grant in January 1865, Confederate vice president Alexander H. Stephens was initially disappointed by Grant's appearance and bearing, his informality of manner and terseness in conversation. After a few days, Stephens came to view Grant as "one of the most remarkable men" he had ever met, although "not aware of his own power." Like others, Stephens found that Grant possessed a mysterious power concealed behind an ordinary facade. Completely in control of himself, Grant was superbly equipped to control others. The power that lies behind Grant's writing gives his *Memoirs* enduring appeal.

John Y. Simon
Southern Illinois University at Carbondale

# GENERAL GRANT BY MATTHEW ARNOLD

WITH

A Rejoinder by Mark Twain

# Introduction

"I THINK I shall do General Grant's *Memoirs*," wrote Matthew Arnold when asked by his nephew to contribute an article to a magazine which he edited. "The Americans will like it. The book has hardly been noticed in England, and Grant is shown by this book to be one of the most solid men they have had. I prefer him to Lincoln. Except Franklin, I hardly know anyone so *selbst-ständig*, so broad and strong-sighted, as well as firm-charactered, that they have had."[1]

Most Americans knew the story of Grant's struggle to write his memoirs. The ex-President and his sons had been swindled, were in debt and without resources, when Grant first attempted to earn money by writing. Even before beginning his memoirs, however, he felt the pain in his throat later diagnosed as a fatal cancer. Unable to speak or eat without frightful pain, Grant raced with death to complete the book which would bring money to support his family. Grant stayed alive by sheer will until he had completed his task.

The first volume of the *Memoirs* was published soon after the national mourning of Grant's death. Mark Twain, who controlled the Charles L. Webster Company, employed an army of agents to sell hundreds of thousands of copies. Even in homes where books were rarely seen, Grant's *Memoirs* stood proudly as a tribute to an American hero.

Matthew Arnold's article dealt with a book respected by Americans whether or not they had read it. Arnold's

1. Arnold to Mrs. Forster, Oct. 21, 1886, George W. E. Russell, ed., *Letters of Matthew Arnold* (London, 1904), III, pp. 299–300.

poetry and essays had been reprinted and widely read in the United States, and he undoubtedly knew that his Grant article would be most carefully read across the Atlantic. Furthermore, as the most influential English literary critic of the day, he would speak with the voice of his nation.

If Arnold hoped to strengthen trans-Atlantic good will, he was to be disappointed; but the result was a graceful tribute to a man Arnold had first met some ten years earlier. After the completion of his second term as President, Grant had embarked on a tour around the world. Although he travelled as a private citizen, his reputation as the best-known American of his day transformed an intended quiet tour into a state visit. On June 18, 1877, Grant was guest of honor at a breakfast in London given by George Smalley, correspondent of the *New York Tribune.* Matthew Arnold was one of the prominent literary and political figures in attendance, and Grant might have been forgiven for not taking much notice of Arnold in a group which included, among others, Robert Browning, Anthony Trollope, Thomas Hughes, and Thomas Henry Huxley.[2]

Arnold's lecture tour in the United States in 1883 was awaited with apprehension by those Americans already familiar with his distaste for democracy, aristocratic prejudices, unorthodox religious views, and fastidious social criticism; he was an exponent of a vague standard of culture which few could understand and none could adopt. On October 22, Arnold was met in New York by Andrew Carnegie, a previous acquaintance, who took him to the first performance at the new Metropolitan Opera House, and installed him in the Windsor Hotel, where Carnegie

2. John Russell Young, *Around the World with General Grant* (New York, 1879), I, pp. 28–29.

himself lived with his mother. At the end of the week, General Grant was a guest at the lavish reception Carnegie gave for Arnold in an octagonal room crammed with celebrities and decorated with garlands of flowers enclosing the titles of Arnold's books.[3]

It was no wonder then, that Grant attended Arnold's first American lecture a few days later at Chickering Hall. The hall was filled beyond capacity and expectant; but Arnold, who would later take some quick elocution lessons in Boston, was unable to make himself heard. "Well, wife," said Grant, "we have paid to see the British lion; we cannot hear him roar, so we had better go home."[4]

The next day, Grant went to the *New York Tribune* office to compliment the report of Arnold's lecture, explaining that he had been unable to hear some important points. "I should not have suspected Grant of either knowing or caring anything whatever about me and my productions," wrote Arnold; but though he found "not much real depth" in this and other manifestations of interest in his lectures, he was obviously delighted.[5]

3. *New York Tribune*, Oct. 28, 1883; Lionel Trilling, *Matthew Arnold* (Rev. ed., New York, 1955), p. 358; Andrew Carnegie, *Autobiography* (Boston and New York, 1920), pp. 298–308. The best account of Arnold's visit is Chilson Hathaway Leonard, "Arnold in America: A Study of Matthew Arnold's Literary Relations with America and of his Visits to this Country in 1883 and 1886," unpublished doctoral dissertation, Yale University, 1932. See Howard Mumford Jones, "Arnold, Aristocracy, and America," *American Historical Review*, XLIX, 3 (April, 1944), 393–409.

4. J. B. Pond, *Eccentricities of Genius* (New York, 1900), p. 323. The *New York Tribune*, *New York Times*, and *New York Herald* of Oct. 31, 1883, were unanimous in declaring the lecture inaudible. The *New York Times*, Nov. 1, 1883, philosophically concluded that people would learn more by reading the printed version of the lecture. Arnold to George W. Smalley, Nov. 27, 1883, *New York Tribune*, May 6, 1888. The essay "Numbers" is included in *Discourses in America* (London and New York, 1896), pp. 1–71.

5. Arnold to sister, Nov. 8, 1883, Russell, *Arnold Letters*, III, p. 142.

Matthew Arnold had written one essay about the United States before his lecture tour, and after the tour he had even more to say. "I find that having been in America wonderfully increases my interest in their men and politics," he remarked.[6] He found the political level higher than he had expected, but social conditions had confirmed his worst expectations. Everywhere he found the mark of the Philistine, and Americans were too sensitive to allow the disclaimer that what he condemned in the United States he fought also in his native land.

An occasional American, like Henry James, would find in Arnold a kindred spirit, but this was rare.[7] Even the American lecture tour, which began pleasantly enough, left behind a senseless controversy with the *Chicago Tribune* and a baseless rumor that Arnold had not given his seat to a lady on a Boston horsecar.[8] Now added to the dislike of an aristocratic Englishman were specific objections to his remarks about American culture.

If the modern American finds in Arnold's essay on General Grant a generous appraisal, his ancestors did not. They could not miss the many passages in which praise for Grant became a reflection on the habits of his countrymen. With ears still ringing with the panegyric provoked by Grant's death less than two years earlier, Americans objected to any qualification in the praise of Grant, and the strongest feelings were caused by the comments on General Grant's grammar by a man whose elegant style they found unpleasant.

6. Arnold to Mrs. Forster, Oct. 18, 1884, Arnold W. Whitredge, ed., *Unpublished Letters of Matthew Arnold* (New Haven, 1923), pp. 54–55.
7. An excellent discussion of American literary reactions to Arnold is available in John Henry Raleigh, *Matthew Arnold and American Culture* (Berkeley, 1957).
8. Leonard, "Arnold in America," pp. 250–53.

A two-part article published in *Murray's Magazine*
would not ordinarily have reached many Americans, but
a Boston publisher reprinted the article in 1887, and in
the following year it was included in a volume containing
all of Arnold's published comments on the United States.[9]
These had sufficient circulation to bring reaction. The
*New York Times* criticized the "bland sense of sufficiency"
with which Arnold discussed the Civil War period. "The
fastidious critic of the elegance and adornments of life,"
thundered the *New York Tribune*, "never seemed to us so
small, so little worth while as when he ranged himself by
the side of this strong and simple patriot-soldier." *The
Literary World* found nothing in the essay save "more
leniency towards the subject than might be expected."[10]
By adding the subtitle, *An Estimate*, to the essay originally
titled *General Grant*, the publishers left Arnold open to
the charge of providing less than promised. James B. Fry,
Provost Marshal General during the Civil War, in an
article in the *North American Review*, attempted to prove
that Grant's writing was superior to that of Arnold, ac-
cused Arnold of distorting Grant's statements, and included an attack upon the policy of the British during the
Civil War.[11]

Fry's anger was slight compared to that of Mark Twain.
It was Twain's proud (though inaccurate) boast that had
he not deserted the Confederate Army early in the war he
would have been among the first rebels captured by

9. Matthew Arnold, *Civilization in the United States: First and
Last Impressions of America* (Boston, 1888).

10. *New York Times*, March 20, 1887; *New York Tribune*, March
1, 1887; *The Literary World*, XVIII, 6 (March 19, 1887), 87; *The
Critic*, XVIII, 7 (May 14, 1887), 243.

11. James B. Fry, "Grant and Matthew Arnold: An Estimate,"
*North American Review*, 144 (April, 1887), 349–57. See Fry, "Mr.
Matthew Arnold on America," *ibid.*, 146 (May, 1888), 515–19.

Grant.[12] Twain was both a personal friend of General Grant and the publisher of his best-selling *Memoirs*.[13] Furthermore, Arnold had singled out Twain for condemnation even before his visit to the United States. "The Quinionian humour of Mr. Mark Twain," he called "attractive to the Philistine of the more gay and light type both here and in America. . . ."[14] When Matthew Arnold visited Boston, he looked for William Dean Howells. When he was told that Howells was currently in Hartford visiting Mark Twain, he exclaimed: "Oh, but he doesn't like *that* sort of thing, does he?"[15] Yet, when Arnold reached Hartford before Howells had left and was introduced by him to Mark Twain at a reception, Arnold and Twain so enjoyed each other's company that Arnold dined the following evening at Twain's home.[16] Twain was at his dazzling best that evening, and while Arnold was walking home with another guest he asked: "And is he *never* serious?" "Mr. Arnold," came the reply, "he is the most serious man in the world."[17]

12. John Gerber, "Mark Twain's 'Private Campaign,'" *Civil War History*, I, 1 (March, 1955), 59–60; Fred W. Lorch, "Mark Twain and the 'Campaign That Failed,'" *American Literature*, XII (Jan., 1941), 463.

13. Twain's recollections of his friendship with Grant are in Albert Bigelow Paine, ed., *Mark Twain's Autobiography* (New York, 1924), I, pp. 13–70; Bernard DeVoto, ed., *Mark Twain in Eruption* (New York, 1940), pp. 170–86; Paine, ed., *Mark Twain's Notebook* (New York, 1935), pp. 174–86; Samuel C. Webster, *Mark Twain: Businessman* (Boston, 1946), *passim*.

14. Arnold, *Civilization in the United States*, p. 92. Quinion appears in *David Copperfield*, chaps. II, X, XI, as manager of the warehouse of Murdstone and Grinby.

15. William Dean Howells, *My Mark Twain* (New York and London, 1910), p. 28.

16. *Ibid.*, p. 29; Henry Nash Smith and William M. Gibson, eds., *Mark Twain-Howells Letters* (Cambridge, Mass., 1960), I, pp. 449–50.

17. Albert Bigelow Paine, *Mark Twain* (New York and London, 1935), II, pp. 758–59.

Arnold failed to understand Twain; after the publication of the essay on Grant, Twain never tried to understand Arnold. Instead, Arnold became a pet prejudice.
Some of the feeling against Arnold was channeled into
*A Connecticut Yankee*, which Twain had already begun,
and a refutation of Arnold's charges against American
newspapers furnishes a long passage in *The American
Claimant*.[18] In the first flush of anger about the Arnold
essay, Twain addressed the annual reunion of the Army
and Navy Club of Connecticut on April 27, 1887, Grant's
birthday.[19] An earlier speaker had declared that Grant
"cared nothing for tactics for the sake of tactics, and doubtless knew nothing of art for art's sake. In his day the task
was not that of spelling beautiful with a big B, but that of
spelling nation with a big N. We Philistines who put our
country before culture have settled that point, and our
leader was a Philistine like ourselves."[20] Borrowing freely
from Fry's article in the current *North American Review*,
Twain delivered his speech. When the great applause for
Twain had died away, the lengthy ceremonies continued.
In the course of his address, Senator Hawley of Connecticut said that he would send a marked copy of Twain's address to his personal friend Matthew Arnold.[21]

Twain's objections to Arnold's essay on Grant may
have been overdone, but they were not lacking in substance. Arnold could not discuss the United States without
an occasional tone of supercilious condescension. Even

18. Louis J. Budd, *Mark Twain, Social Philosopher* (Blooming-
ton, Indiana, 1962), pp. 118–20; Raleigh, *Arnold and American
Culture*, pp. 64–65; John B. Hoben, "Mark Twain's A Connecticut
Yankee: A Genetic Study," *American Literature*, XVIII (Nov.,
1946), 197–218; Mark Twain, *The American Claimant*, chap. X.
19. *New York Tribune, New York World*, April 28, 1887.
20. M. B. Riddle, *Hartford Courant*, April 28, 1887.
21. *Ibid.*

the most ardent of Arnold's American friends winced when he claimed that he began to read Lincoln's Gettysburg Address, but stopped at the Americanism of "dedicated to the proposition."[22]

Those who had known Grant over the years found Arnold's essay an oversimplification. As Henry Adams remarked, "One seemed to know him so well, and really knew so little."[23] Photographs of Grant often bring out different characteristics: the sensitivity or the self-assurance, the strength or the tenderness, the bulldog look or a diffused melancholy. Arnold missed many of the complexities of Grant, but, like the photographers, he had a true likeness.

22. William E. Barton, *Lincoln at Gettysburg* (New York, 1950), p. 146.

23. *The Education of Henry Adams* (Boston and New York, 1918), p. 263.

# General Grant by Matthew Arnold

## PART I.

I HAVE HEARD it said, I know not with what degree of truth, that while the sale in America of General Grant's *Personal Memoirs* has produced three hundred thousand dollars for the benefit of his widow and family, there have not in England been sold of the book three hundred copies.[1] Certainly the book has had no wide circulation here, it has not been much read or much discussed. There are obvious reasons for this. The book relates in great detail the military history of the American Civil War, so far as Grant bore part in it; such a history cannot possibly have for other nations the interest which it has for the United States themselves. For the general reader, outside of America, it certainly cannot; as to the value and importance of the history to the military specialist, that is a question on which I hear very conflicting opinions expressed, and one on which I myself can have, of course, no opinion to offer. So far as the general European reader might still be attracted to such a history, in spite of its military details, for the sake of the importance of the issues at stake and of the personages engaged, we in Europe have, it cannot be denied, in approaching an American recital of the deeds of "the greatest nation upon earth," some apprehension and mistrust to get over. We may be pardoned for doubting whether we shall in the recital find measure, whether we shall find sobriety. Then, too, General Grant, the central figure of these *Memoirs*, is not to the English imagination the hero of the American Civil War; the hero

1. Total payments to the Grant family may have reached $450,000. All numbered notes have been added by the editor.

[ 11 ]

is Lee, and of Lee the *Memoirs* tell us little. Moreover General Grant, when he was in England, did not himself personally interest people much. Later he fell in America into the hands of financing speculators, and his embarrassments, though they excited sorrow and compassion, did not at all present themselves to us as those of "a good man struggling with adversity." For all these reasons, then, the *Personal Memoirs* have in England been received with coldness and indifference.

I, too, had seen General Grant in England, and did not find him interesting. If I said the truth, I should say that I thought him ordinary-looking, dull and silent. An expression of gentleness and even sweetness in the eyes, which the portraits in the *Memoirs* show, escaped me. A strong, resolute, business-like man, who by possession of unlimited resources in men and money, and by the unsparing use of them, had been enabled to wear down and exhaust the strength of the South, this was what I supposed Grant to be, this and little more.

Some documents published by General Badeau in the American newspapers first attracted my serious attention to Grant.[2] Among those documents was a letter from him which showed qualities for which, in the rapid and uncharitable view which our cursory judgments of men so often take, I had by no means given him credit. It was the letter of a man with the virtue, rare everywhere, but more rare in America, perhaps, than anywhere else, the virtue of being able to confront and resist popular clamour, the *civium ardor prava jubentium*. Public opinion seemed in favour of a hard and insolent course, the authorities

2. Badeau, formerly Grant's secretary, published so much in the newspapers that it is impossible to pinpoint Arnold's reference. Grant's correspondence with Badeau is available in Adam Badeau, *Grant in Peace: From Appomattox to Mount McGregor* (Hartford, Conn., 1887), chap. L.

seemed putting pressure upon Grant to make him follow it. He resisted with firmness and dignity. After reading that letter I turned to General Grant's *Personal Memoirs*, then just published. This man, I said to myself, deserves respect and attention; and I read the two bulky volumes through.

I found shown in them a man, strong, resolute and business-like, as Grant had appeared to me when I first saw him; a man with no magical personality, touched by no divine light and giving out none. I found a language all astray in its use of *will* and *shall*, *should* and *would*, an English employing the verb *to conscript* and the participle *conscripting*, and speaking in a despatch to the Secretary of War of having *badly whipped* the enemy; an English without charm and without high breeding. But at the same time I found a man of sterling good-sense as well as of the firmest resolution; a man, withal, humane, simple, modest; from all restless self-consciousness and desire for display perfectly free; never boastful where he himself was concerned, and where his nation was concerned seldom boastful, boastful only in circumstances where nothing but high genius or high training, I suppose, can save an American from being boastful. I found a language straightforward, nervous, firm, possessing in general the high merit of saying clearly in the fewest possible words what had to be said, and saying it, frequently, with shrewd and unexpected turns of expression. The *Memoirs* renewed and completed the impression which the letter given by General Badeau had made upon me. And now I want to enable Grant and his *Memoirs* as far as possible to speak for themselves to the English public, which knows them, I believe, as imperfectly as a few months ago I myself did.

General Grant was born at Point Pleasant, in the State

of Ohio, on the 27th of April, 1822. His name, *Ulysses*, makes one think of *Tristram Shandy*; but how often do American names make one think of *Tristram Shandy*! The father of the little Ulysses followed the trade of a tanner; he was a constant reader both of books and newspapers, and "before he was twenty years of age was a constant contributor," his son tells us, "to Western newspapers, and was also, from that time, until he was fifty years old, an able debater in the societies for this purpose, which were then common in the West."[3] Of many and many an American farmer and tradesman this is the history. General Grant, however, never shared the paternal and national love for public speaking. As to his schooling, he never, he tells us, missed a quarter from school, from the time he was old enough to attend till the time when he left home, at the age of seventeen, for the Military Academy at West Point. But the instruction in the country schools at that time was very poor:—

"A single teacher—who was often a man or a woman incapable of teaching much, even if they imparted all they knew—would have thirty or forty scholars, male and female, from the infant learning the A B C, up to the young lady of eighteen and the boy of twenty studying the highest branches taught—the three R's. I never saw an algebra, or other mathematical work higher than the arithmetic, until after I was appointed to West Point. I then bought a work on algebra in Cincinnati; but, having no teacher, it was Greek to me."

This schooling is unlike that of our young gentlemen preparing for Sandhurst or Woolwich, but still more unlike theirs is Grant's life out of school-hours. He has told

3. In quoting the *Memoirs*, Arnold sometimes altered the spelling to conform to British usage and sometimes altered the punctuation. The extracts are, however, substantially accurate.

us how regularly he attended his school, such as it was. He proceeds:

"This did not exempt me from labour. In my early days, every one laboured more or less in the region where my youth was spent, and more in proportion to their private means. It was only the very poor who were exempt. While my father carried on the manufacture of leather and worked at the trade himself, he owned and tilled considerable land. I detested the trade, preferring almost any other labour; but I was fond of agriculture and of all employments in which horses were used. We had, among other lands, fifty acres of forest within a mile of the village. In the fall of the year choppers were employed to cut enough wood to last a twelvemonth. When I was seven or eight years of age I began hauling all the wood used in the house and shops. I could not load it on the wagons, of course, at that time, but I could drive, and the choppers would load and some one at the house unload. When about eleven years old, I was strong enough to hold a plough. From that age until seventeen I did all the work done with horses, such as breaking up the land, furrowing, ploughing corn and potatoes, bringing in the crops when harvested, hauling all the wood, besides tending two or three horses, a cow or two, and sawing wood for stoves, &c., while still attending school. For this I was compensated by the fact that there never was any scolding or punishing by my parents: no objection to rational enjoyments, such as fishing, going to the creek a mile away to swim in summer; taking a horse and visiting my grandparents in the adjoining county, fifteen miles off; skating on the ice in winter, or taking a horse and sleigh when there was snow on the ground."

The bringing up of Abraham Lincoln was also, I suppose, much on this wise; and meagre, too meagre, as may have been the schooling, I confess I am inclined on the whole to exclaim: "What a wholesome bringing up it was!"

I must find room for one story of Grant's boyhood, a story which he tells against himself:—

"There was a Mr. Ralston living within a few miles of the village, who owned a colt that I very much wanted. My father had offered twenty dollars for it, but Ralston wanted twenty-five. I was so anxious to have the colt, that, after the owner left, I begged to be allowed to take him at the price demanded. My father yielded, but said twenty dollars was all the horse was worth, and told me to offer that price; if it was not accepted, I might offer twenty-two and a half, and if that would not get him, might give the twenty-five. I at once mounted a horse and went for the colt. When I got to Mr. Ralston's house, I said to him: 'Papa says I may offer you twenty dollars for the colt, but if you won't take that, I am to offer twenty-two and a half, and if you won't take that, to give you twenty-five.' It would not require a Connecticut man to guess the price finally agreed upon. I could not have been over eight years old at the time. This transaction caused me great heart-burning. The story got amongst the boys of the village, and it was a long time before I heard the last of it."

The boys of the village may well have been amused. How astounding to find an American boy so little "'cute," so little "smart." But how delightful also, and how refreshing; how full of promise for the boy's future character! Grant came in later life to see straight and to see clear, more than most men, more than even most Americans, whose virtue it is that in matters within their range they see straight and see clear; but he never was in the least "smart," and it is one of his merits.

The United States Senator for Ohio procured for young

Grant, when he was seventeen years old, a nomination to West Point.[4] He was not himself eager for it. His father one day said to him: "Ulysses, I believe you are going to receive the appointment." "What appointment?" I enquired. "To West Point; I have applied for it." "But I won't go," I said. He said he thought I would, *and I thought so too, if he did*. I really had no objection to going to West Point, except that I had a very exalted idea of the acquirements necessary to get through. I did not believe I possessed them, and could not bear the idea of failing."

He did go. Although he had no military ardour he desired to see the world. Already he had seen more of it than most of the boys of his village; he had visited Cincinnati, the principal city of his native State, and Louisville, the principal city of the adjoining State of Kentucky; he had also been out as far as Wheeling in Virginia, and now, if he went to West Point, he would have the opportunity of seeing Philadelphia and New York. "When these places were visited," he says, "I would have been glad to have had a steamboat or railroad collision, or any other accident happen, by which I might have received a temporary injury sufficient to make me ineligible for awhile to enter the Academy." He took his time on the road, and having left home in the middle of May, did not arrive at West Point until the end of the month. Two weeks later he passed his examination for admission, very much, he tells us, to his surprise. But none of his professional studies interested him, though he did well in mathematics, which he found, he says, very easy to him. Throughout his first year he found the life tedious, read novels, and had no intention of remaining in the army, even if he should succeed in

4. The actual appointment was secured through Thomas L. Hamer, a member of the House of Representatives. Lloyd Lewis, *Captain Sam Grant* (Boston, 1950), pp. 56–57.

graduating at the end of his four years' course, a success which he did not expect to attain. When in 1839 a Bill was discussed in Congress for abolishing the Military Academy, he hoped the Bill might pass, and so set him free. But it did not pass, and a year later he would have been sorry, he says, if it had passed, although he still found his life at West Point dull. His last two years went quicker than his first two; but they still seemed to him "about five times as long as Ohio years." At last all his examinations were passed, he was appointed to an infantry regiment, and, before joining, went home on leave with a desperate cough and a stature which had run up too fast for his strength.

In September 1843 he joined his regiment, the 4th United States infantry, at Jefferson Barracks, St. Louis. No doubt his training at West Point, an establishment with a public and high standing, and with serious studies, had been invaluable to him. But still he had no desire to remain in the army. At St. Louis he met and became attached to a young lady whom he afterwards married, Miss Dent, and his hope was to become an assistant professor of mathematics at West Point. With this hope he re-read at Jefferson Barracks his West Point mathematics, and pursued a course of historical study also. But the Mexican war came on and kept him in the army.

With the annexation of Texas in prospect, Grant's regiment was moved to Fort Jessup on the western border of Louisiana. Ostensibly the American troops were to prevent filibustering into Texas; really they were sent as a menace to Mexico in case she appeared to contemplate war. Grant's life in Louisiana was pleasant. He had plenty of professional duty, many of his brother officers having been detailed on special duty away from the regiment. He gave up the thought of becoming a teacher of mathematics, and read only for his own amusement, "and not very much for that"; he kept a horse and rode, visited the planters on the Red River; and was out of doors the whole day nearly; and so he quite recovered from the cough, and the threatenings of consumption, which he had carried with him from West Point. "I have often thought," he adds, "that my life was saved, and my health restored, by exercise and exposure enforced by an administrative act and a war, both of which I disapproved."

For disapprove the menace to Mexico, and the subsequent war, he did. One lingers over a distinguished man's days of growth and formation, so important for all which is to come after. And already, under young Grant's plain exterior and air of indifference, there had grown up in him an independent and sound judgment. "Generally the officers of the army were indifferent whether the annexation was consummated or not; but not so all of them. For myself, I was bitterly opposed to the measure, and to this day regard the war which resulted as one of the most unjust ever waged by a stronger against a weaker nation."

Texas was annexed, a territory larger than the Austrian Empire; and after taking military possession of Texas, the American army of occupation, under General Taylor, went on and occupied some more disputed territory beyond. Even here they did not stop, but went further on still, meaning apparently to force the Mexicans to attack them and begin war. "We were sent to provoke war, but it was essential that Mexico should commence it. It was very doubtful whether Congress would declare war; but if Mexico should attack our troops, the Executive could announce: 'Whereas war exists by the acts of, etc.,' and prosecute the contest with vigour. Once initiated, there were few public men who would have the courage to oppose it."

Incensed at the Americans fortifying themselves on the

Rio Grande, opposite Matamoras, the Mexicans at last fired the necessary shot, and the war was commenced. This was in March 1846. In September 1847 the American army entered the city of Mexico. Vera Cruz, Puebla, and other principal cities of the country, were already in their possession. In February 1848 was signed the treaty which gave to the United States Texas with the Rio Grande for its boundary, and the whole territory then included in New Mexico and Upper California. For New Mexico and California, however, the Americans paid a sum of fifteen millions of dollars.

Grant marks with sagacity and justness the causes and effects of the Mexican war. As the North grew in numbers and population, the South required more territory to counterbalance it; to maintain through this wide territory the institution of slavery, it required to have control of the national Government. With great energy and ability, it obtained this control; it acquired Texas and other large regions for slavery; it proceeded to use the powers of Government, in the North as well as in the South, for the purpose of securing and maintaining its hold upon its slaves. But the wider the territory over which slavery was spread, and the more numerous the slaves, the greater became the difficulty of making this hold quite secure, and the stronger grew the irritation of the North to see the powers and laws of the whole nation used for the purpose. The Fugitive Slave Law brought this irritation to its height, made it uncontrollable, and the War of Secession was the result. "The Southern rebellion," says Grant, "was largely the outgrowth of the Mexican war. Nations, like individuals, are punished for their transgressions. We got our punishment in the most sanguinary and expensive war of modern times."

The part of Grant in the Mexican war was of course that

of a young subaltern only, and is described by him with characteristic modesty. He showed, however, of what good stuff he was made, and his performances with a certain howitzer in a church-steeple so pleased his general that he sent for Grant, commended him, and ordered a second howitzer to be placed at his disposal. A captain of voltigeurs came with the gun in charge. "I could not tell the general," says Grant, "that there was not room enough in the steeple for another gun, because he probably would have looked upon such a statement as a contradiction from a second lieutenant. I took the captain with me, but did not use his gun."

When the evacuation of Mexico was completed, Grant married, in August 1848, Miss Julia Dent, to whom he had been engaged more than four years. For two years the young couple lived at Detroit in Michigan, where Grant was now stationed; he was then ordered to the Pacific coast. It was settled that Mrs. Grant should, during his absence, live with her own family at St. Louis. The regiment went first to Aspinwall, then to California and Oregon. In 1853 Grant became captain. But he had now two children, and saw no chance of supporting his family on his pay as an army officer. He determined to resign, and in the following year he did so. He left the Pacific coast, he tells us, very much attached to it, and with the full intention of one day making his home there, an intention which he did not abandon until, in the winter of 1863–4, Congress passed the Act appointing him Lieutenant-General of the armies of the United States.

His life on leaving the army offers, like his early training, a curious contrast to what usually takes place amongst ourselves. First he tried farming, on a farm belonging to his wife near St. Louis; but he could not make it answer, though he worked hard. He had insufficient capital, and more than sufficient fever and ague. After four years he established a partnership with a cousin of his wife named Harry Boggs, in a real estate agency business in St. Louis. He found that the business was not more than one person could do, and not enough to support two families. So he withdrew from the co-partnership with Boggs, and in May 1860 removed to Galena, Illinois, and took a clerkship in a leather shop there belonging to his father.

Politics now began to interest him, and his reflexions on them at the moment when the War of Secession was approaching I must quote:

"Up to the Mexican war there were a few out and out abolitionists, men who carried their hostility to slavery into all elections, from those for a justice of the peace up to the Presidency of the United States. They were noisy but not numerous. But the great majority of people at the North, where slavery did not exist, were opposed to the institution, and looked upon its existence in any part of the country as unfortunate. They did not hold the States where slavery existed responsible for it, and believed that protection should be given to the right of property in slaves until some satisfactory way could be reached to be rid of the institution. Opposition to slavery was a creed of neither political party. But with the inauguration of the Mexican war, in fact with the annexation of Texas, the inevitable conflict commenced. As the time for the Presidential election of 1856—the first at which I had the opportunity of voting—approached, party feeling began to run high."

Grant himself voted in 1856 for Buchanan, the candidate of the Slave States, because he saw clearly, he says, that in the exasperation of feeling at that time, the election of a Republican President meant the secession of all the Slave States, and the plunging of the country into a war of which no man could foretell the issue. He hoped that in the course of the next four years—the Slave States having got a President of their own choice, and being without a pretext for secession—men's passions would quiet down, and the catastrophe be averted. Even if it was not, he thought the country would by that time be better prepared to receive the shock and to resist it.

I am not concerned to discuss Grant's reasons for his vote, but I wish to remark how completely his reflexions dispose of the reproaches addressed so often by Americans to England for not sympathizing with the North attacking slavery, in a war with the South upholding it. From what he says it is evident how very far the North was, when the war began, from attacking slavery. Grant himself was not for attacking it; Lincoln was not. They, and the North in general, wished "that protection should be given to the right of property in slaves, until some satisfactory way could be reached to be rid of the institution." England took the North at its word, and regarded its struggle as one for preserving the Union, and the force and greatness which accrue from the Union, not for abolishing slavery. True, far-sighted people here might perceive that the war must probably issue, if the North prevailed, in the abolition of slavery, and might wish well to the North on that account. They did so; coldly, it is true, for the attitude of the North was not such as to call forth enthusiasm, but sincerely. A great number of people in England, on the other hand, looking at the surface of things merely, clearly seeing that the North was not meaning to attack slavery but to uphold the power and grandeur of the United States, thought themselves quite free to wish well to the South, the weaker side which was making a gallant fight, and to favour the breaking up of the Union.

Here was the real offence. The Americans of the North, admiring and valuing their great Republic above all things, could not forgive disfavour or coldness to it; could only impute them to envy and jealousy. Far-sighted people in England might perceive that the maintenance of the Union was not only likely to bring about the emancipation of the slave, but was also on other grounds to be desired for the good of the world. Our artizans might be in sympathy with the popular and unaristocratic institutions of the United States, and be therefore averse to any weakening of the great Republic. And these feelings prevailed here, as is well known, so as to govern the course taken by this country during the War of Secession. Still, there was much disfavour, and more coldness. Americans were, and are, indignant that the upholding of their great Republic should have had in England such cold friends, and so many actual enemies. It is like the indignant astonishment of George Sand during the German war, "to see Europe looking on with indifference to the danger of such a civilization as that of France." But admiration and favour are uncompellable; we admire and favour only an object which delights us, helps us, elevates us, and does us good. The thing is to make us feel that the object does this. Self-admiration and self-laudation will not convince us; on the contrary, they indispose us. France would be more attractive to us if she were less prone to call herself the head of civilization and the pride of the world; the United States, if they were more backward in proclaiming themselves "the greatest nation upon earth."

In 1860 Lincoln was elected President, and the catastrophe, which Grant hoped might have been averted, arrived. He had in 1860 no vote, but things were now come to that pass that he felt compelled to make his choice between minority rule and rule by the majority, and he was glad, therefore, to see Lincoln elected.[5] Secession was imminent, and with secession, war; but Grant confesses that his own views at that time were those officially expressed later on by Mr. Seward, that "the war would be over in ninety days." He retained these views, he tells us, until after the battle of Shiloh.

Lincoln was not to come into office until the spring of 1861. The South was confident and defiant, and in the North there were prominent men and newspapers declaring that the government had no legal right to coerce the South. It was unsafe for Mr. Lincoln, when he went to be sworn into office in March 1861, to travel as President-elect; he had to be smuggled into Washington. When he took on the 4th of March his oath of office to maintain the Union, eleven States had gone out of it.[6] On the 11th of April, Fort Sumter in Charleston harbour was fired upon, and a few days after was captured. Then the President issued a call for 75,000 men. "There was not a State in the North of a million inhabitants," says Grant, "that would not have furnished the entire number faster than arms could have been supplied to them, if it had been necessary."

As soon as news of the call for volunteers reached Galena, where Grant lived, the citizens were summoned to meet at the Court House in the evening. The Court House was crammed. Grant, though a comparative stranger, was called upon to preside, because he had been

5. Grant says that his "pledges would have compelled me to vote for Stephen A. Douglas, who had no possible chance of election. The contest was really between Mr. Breckinridge and Mr. Lincoln . . . I wanted, as between these candidates, to see Mr. Lincoln elected." *Personal Memoirs of U. S. Grant* (New York, 1885–86), I, p. 216.

6. At the time of Lincoln's inauguration, seven states had seceded, and four others followed after Fort Sumter. The *Memoirs* (I, p. 229) do not make the sequence of secession clear.

in the army, and had seen service. "With much embarrassment and some prompting, I made out to announce the
object of the meeting." Speeches followed; then volunteers were called for to form the company which Galena
had to furnish. The company was raised, and the officers
and non-commissioned officers were elected, before the
meeting adjourned. Grant declined the captaincy before
the balloting, but promised to help them all he could, and
to be found in the service, in some position, if there should
actually be war. "I never," he adds, "went into our
leather store after that meeting, to put up a package or do
other business."

After seeing the company mustered at Springfield, the
capital of Illinois, Grant, was asked by the Governor of the
State to give some help in the military office, where his old
army experience enabled him to be of great use. But on
the 24th of May he wrote to the Adjutant-General of the
Army, saying that, "having been fifteen years in the regu-
lar army, including four at West Point, and feeling it the
duty of every one who has been educated at the Government expense to offer their services for the support of the
Government," he wished to tender his services until the
close of the war, "in such capacity as may be offered." He
got no answer. He then thought of getting appointed on
the staff of General McClellan, whom he had known at
West Point, and went to seek the General at Cincinnati.
He called twice, but failed to see him. While he was at
Cincinnati, however, the President issued his second call
for troops, this time for 300,000 men; and the Governor of
Illinois, mindful of Grant's recent help, appointed him
colonel of the 21st Illinois regiment of infantry. In a
month he had brought his regiment into a good state of
drill and discipline, and was then ordered to a point on a
railroad in Missouri, where an Illinois regiment was sur-

rounded by "rebels." His own account of his first experience as a Commander is very characteristic of him:

"My sensations as we approached what I supposed might
be 'a field of battle,' were anything but agreeable. I had
been in all the engagements in Mexico that it was possible
for one person to be in; but not in command. If some one
else had been colonel, and I had been lieutenant-colonel,
I do not think I would have felt any trepidation. Before
we were prepared to cross the Mississippi River at Quincy,
my anxiety was relieved; for the men of the besieged regiment came straggling into the town. I am inclined to think
both sides got frightened and ran away."

Now, however, he was started; and from this time until
he received Lee's surrender at Appomattox Court House,
four years later, he was always the same strong man,
showing the same valuable qualities. He had not the
pathos and dignity of Lee, his power of captivating the admiring interest, almost the admiring affection, of his pro-
fession and of the world. He had not the fire, the celerity,
the genial cordiality of Sherman, whose person and manner emitted a *ray* (to adopt, with a very slight change,
Lamb's well-known lines)—

> "a ray
> Which struck a cheer upon the day,
> A cheer which would not go away—"

Grant had not these. But he certainly had a good deal of
the character and qualities which we so justly respect in
the Duke of Wellington. Wholly free from show, parade,
and pomposity; sensible and sagacious; scanning closely
the situation, seeing things as they actually were, then
making up his mind as to the right thing to be done under
the circumstances, and doing it; never flurried, never
vacillating, but also not stubborn, able to reconsider and

change his plans, a man of resource; when, however, he had really fixed on the best course to take, the right nail to drive, resolutely and tenaciously persevering, driving the nail hard home—Grant was all this, and surely in all this he resembles the Duke of Wellington.

The eyes of Europe, during the War of Secession, were chiefly fixed on the conflict in the East. Grant, however, as we have seen, began his career, not on the great and conspicuous stage of the East, but in the West. He did not come to the East until, by taking Vicksburg, he had attracted all eyes to the West, and to the course of events there.

We have seen how Grant's first expedition in command ended. The second ended in much the same way, and is related by him with the same humour. He was ordered to move against a Colonel Thomas Harris, encamped on the Salt River. As Grant and his men approached the place where they expected to find Harris, "my heart," he says, "kept getting higher and higher, until it felt to me as if it was in my throat." But when they reached the point from which they looked down into the valley where they supposed Harris to be, behold, Harris was gone! "My heart resumed its place. It occurred to me at once that Harris had been as much afraid of me as I had been of him. This was a view of the question I had never taken before, but I never forgot it afterwards. I never forgot that an enemy had as much reason to fear my forces as I had his. The lesson was valuable."

But already he inspired confidence. Shortly after his return from the Salt River, the President asked the Congressmen from Illinois to recommend seven citizens of that State for the rank of brigadier-general, and the Congressmen unanimously recommended Grant first on the list. In August he was appointed to the command of a district, and on the 4th of September assumed command at Cairo, where the Ohio River joins the Mississippi. His first important success was to seize and fortify Paducah, an important post at the mouth of the Tennessee River, about fifty miles from Cairo. By the 1st of November he had 20,000 well-drilled men under his command. In November he fought a smart action at Belmont, on the western bank of the Mississippi, with the object of preventing the Confederates who were in strong force at Columbus in Kentucky, on the eastern bank, from detaching troops to the West. He succeeded in his object, and his troops, who came under fire for the first time, behaved well. Grant himself had a horse shot under him.

Very important posts to the Confederates were Fort Henry on the Tennessee and Fort Donelson on the Cumberland River. Grant thought he could capture Fort Henry. He went to St. Louis to see General Halleck, whose subordinate he was, and to state his plan. "I was received with so little cordiality that I perhaps stated the object of my visit with less clearness than I might have done, and I had not uttered many sentences before I was cut short as if my plan was preposterous. I returned to Cairo very much crest-fallen."

He persevered, however, and after consulting with the officer commanding the gunboats at Cairo, he renewed, by telegraph, the suggestion that, if permitted, he "could take and hold Fort Henry on the Tennessee." This time he was backed by the officer in command of the gunboats. Next day, he wrote fully to explain his plan. In two days he received instructions from headquarters to move upon Fort Henry, and on the 2nd of February, 1862, the expedition started.

He took Fort Henry on the 6th of February, and announcing his success to General Halleck, informed him that he would now take Fort Donelson. On the 16th, Fort Donelson surrendered, and Grant made nearly 15,000 prisoners. There was delight in the North, depression at Richmond. Grant was at once promoted to be major-general of volunteers. He thought, both then and ever after, that by the fall of Fort Donelson the way was opened to the forces of the North all over the south-west without much resistance, that a vigorous commander, disposing of all the troops west of the Alleghanies, might have at once marched to Chattanooga, Corinth, Memphis, and Vicksburg, and broken down every resistance. There was no such commander, and time was given to the enemy to collect armies and fortify new positions.

The next point for attack was Corinth, at the junction of the two most important railroads in the Mississippi Valley. After Grant had, after a hard and bloody struggle of two days, won the battle of Shiloh, in which a ball cut in two the scabbard of his sword, and more than 10,000 men were killed and wounded on the side of the North, General Halleck, who did not love Grant, arrived on the scene of action and assumed the command. "Although next to him in rank," says Grant, "and nominally in command of my old district and army, I was ignored as much as if I had been at the most distant point of territory within my jurisdiction." On the advance to Corinth, "I was little more than an observer. Orders were sent direct to the right wing or reserve, ignoring me, and advances were made from one line of intrenchments to another without notifying me. My position was so embarrassing, in fact, that I made several applications to be relieved." When he suggested a movement, he was silenced. Presently the Confederate troops evacuated Corinth in safety, carrying with them all public property. On the side of the North, there was much disappointment at the slackness with which the enemy had been pressed, and at his success in saving his entire army.

But Corinth was evacuated; the naval forces of the North took Memphis, and now held the Mississippi River from its source to that point; New Orleans and Baton Rouge had fallen into their possession. The Confederates at the West were now narrowed down, for all communication with Richmond, to the single line of road running east from Vicksburg. To dispossess them of Vicksburg, therefore, was of the highest importance. At this point I must stop for the present. Public attention was not yet fixed upon Grant, as it became after his success at Vicksburg; and with his success there a second chapter of his life opens. But already he had shown his talent for succeeding. Cardinal Mazarin used to ask concerning a man before employing him, *Est-il heureux?* Grant was *heureux*.

## PART II.*

WE LEFT Grant projecting his attack upon Vicksburg. In the autumn of 1862, the second year of the war, the prospect for the North appeared gloomy. The Confederates were further advanced than at the beginning of the struggle. Many loyal people, says Grant, despaired at that time of ever saving the Union; President Lincoln never himself lost faith in the final triumph of the Northern cause, but the administration at Washington was uneasy and anxious. The elections of 1862 had gone against the party which was for prosecuting the war at all costs and at all risks until the Union was saved. Voluntary enlistments had ceased; to fill the ranks of the Northern armies the draft had been resorted to. Unless a great success came to restore the spirit of the North, it seemed probable that the draft would be resisted, that men would begin to desert, and that the power to capture and punish deserters would be lost. It was Grant's conviction that there was nothing left to be done but *"to go forward to a decisive victory."*

At first, however, after the battle of Shiloh and the taking of Corinth, he could accomplish little. General Halleck, his chief, appears to have been at this time ill-disposed to him, and to have treated him with coldness and incivility. In July 1862, General Halleck was appointed general-in-chief of all the armies of the North, with his headquarters in Washington, and Grant remained in Tennessee in chief command. But his army

*Personal Memoirs of U. S. Grant (2 vols.; Sampson Low, Marston, & Co.).

suffered such depletion by detaching men to defend long lines of communication, to repair ruined railroads, to reinforce generals in need of succour, that he found himself entirely on the defensive in a hostile territory. Nevertheless in a battle fought to protect Corinth he repulsed the enemy with great slaughter, and being no longer anxious for the safety of the territory within his command, and having been reinforced, he resolved on a forward movement against Vicksburg.

Vicksburg occupies the first high ground on the Mississippi below Memphis. Communication between the parts of the Confederacy divided by the Mississippi was through Vicksburg. So long as the Confederates held Vicksburg, and Port Hudson lower down, the free navigation of the river was prevented. The fall of Vicksburg, as the event proved, was sure to bring with it the fall of Port Hudson also. Grant saw nearly his whole force absorbed in holding the railway lines north of Vicksburg; he considered that if he moved forward, driving the enemy before him into Southern territory not as yet subdued, those lines in his rear would almost hold themselves, and most of his force would be free for field operations. But in moving forward he moved further from his bases of supplies. One of these was at Holly Springs, in the north of the State of Mississippi; the enemy appeared there, captured the garrison, and destroyed all the stores of food, forage, and munitions of war. This loss taught Grant a lesson by which he, and Sherman after him, profited greatly: the lesson that in a wide and productive country, such as that in which he was operating, to cling to a distant base of supply was not necessary; the country he was in would afford the supplies needed. He was amazed, he says, when he was compelled by the loss of Holly Springs to collect supplies in the country immediately around him, at the abundant quantity which the country afforded. He found that after leaving two months' supplies for the use of the families whose stores were taken, he could, off the region where he was, have subsisted his army for a period four times as long as he had actually to remain there. Later in the campaign he took full advantage of the experience thus gained.

The fleet under Admiral Porter co-operated with him, but all endeavours to capture Vicksburg from the north were unavailing. The Mississippi winds and winds through its rich alluvial valley; the country is intersected by *bayous* or water-courses filled from the river, with overhanging trees and with narrow and tortuous channels, where the bends could not be turned by a vessel of any length. To cross this country in the face of an enemy was impossible. The problem was to get in rear of the object of attack, and to secure a footing upon dry ground on the high or eastern side of the Mississippi—the side on which Vicksburg stands—for operating against the place. On the 30th of January, 1863, Grant, having left Memphis, took the command at Young's Point in Louisiana, on the western bank of the Mississippi, not far above Vicksburg, bent on solving the problem.

It was a wet country and a wet winter, with high water in the Mississippi and its tributaries. The troops encamped on the river bank had, in order to be out of the water, to occupy the levees, or dykes, along the river edge, and the ground immediately behind. This gave so limited a space, that one corps of Grant's army, when he assumed the command at Young's Point, was at Lake Providence, seventy miles above Vicksburg. The troops suffered much from malarial fevers and other sickness, but the hospital arrangements were excellent.

Four ineffectual attempts were in the course of the

winter made to get at the object of attack by various routes. Grant, meanwhile, was maturing his plan. His plan was to traverse the peninsula where he lay encamped, then to cross the Mississippi, and thus to be able to attack Vicksburg from the south and east. Above Young's Point, at Milliken's Bend, begins a series of bayous, forming, as it were, the chord of an immense bend of the Mississippi, and falling into the river some fifty miles below Vicksburg. Behind the levees bordering these bayous were tolerable roads, by which, as soon as they emerged from the waters, Grant's troops and wagon-trains could cross the peninsula. The difficulties were indeed great: four bridges had to be built across wide bayous, and the rapid fall of the waters increased the current, and made bridge-building troublesome; but at work of this kind the "Yankee soldier" is in his element. By the 24th of April Grant had his headquarters at the southern extremity of the bend. The navy under Admiral Porter, escorting steamers and barges to serve as ferries and for the transport of supplies, had run fourteen miles of batteries, passed Vicksburg, and come down the river to join Grant. A further march of twenty-two miles was still necessary in order to reach the first high ground, where the army might land and establish itself on the eastern shore. This first high land is at Grand Gulf, a place strongly held at that time by the Confederates, and as unattackable from the river as Vicksburg itself. Porter ran the batteries of Grand Gulf as he had run those of Vicksburg; the army descended the river a few miles, and on the 30th of April was landed at Bruinsburg, on the eastern shore, without meeting an enemy.

Grant's plan had succeeded. He was established on the eastern bank, below and in rear of Vicksburg. Though Vicksburg was not yet taken, and though he was in the enemy's country, with a vast river and the stronghold of

Vicksburg between him and his base of supplies, yet he "felt a degree of relief scarcely ever equalled, since I was on dry ground on the same side of the river with the enemy."

And indeed from this moment his success was continuous. The enemy had at Grand Gulf, at Haines Bluff north of Vicksburg, and at Jackson, the capital of the State of Mississippi, in which State all these places are, about 60,000 men. After fighting and losing an action to cover Grand Gulf, the Confederates evacuated that place, and Grant occupied it on the 3rd of May. By the 7th of May Sherman joined him at Grand Gulf, and he found himself with a force of 33,000 men. He then determined at once to attack the enemy's forces in the rear of Vicksburg, and then to move on the stronghold itself. In order to use Grand Gulf as his base of supplies for these operations, he must have constructed additional roads, and this would have been a work of time. He determined therefore merely to bring up by the single road available from Grand Gulf, what rations of biscuit, coffee, and salt he could, and to make the country he traversed furnish everything else. Beef, mutton, poultry, molasses, and forage were to be found, he knew, in abundance. The cautious Halleck would be sure to disapprove this bold plan of almost abandoning the base of supplies, but Grant counted on being able to obtain his object before he could be interfered with from Washington.

The nature of the ground making Vicksburg easily defensible on the south, Grant determined to get on the railroad running east from Vicksburg to Jackson, the State capital, and to approach the stronghold from that side. At Jackson was a strong Confederate force, the city was an important railway centre, and all supplies of men and stores for Vicksburg came thence; this source of aid had to be stopped. But in order to reach Jackson, Grant had to abandon even that one road by which he had partially supplied his army hitherto, to cut loose from his base of supplies altogether. He did so without hesitation. After a successful action he entered Jackson on the 14th of May, driving out of it the Confederates under General Johnston, and destroyed the place in so far as it was a railroad centre and a manufactory of military supplies. Then he turned westward, and after a severe battle shut up Pemberton in Vicksburg. An assault on Pemberton's defences was unsuccessful, but Vicksburg was closely invested. Pemberton's stores began to run short, Johnston was unable to come to his relief, and on the 4th of July, Independence Day, he surrendered Vicksburg, with its garrison of nearly thirty-two thousand men, ordnance and stores. As Grant had foreseen, Port Hudson surrendered as soon as the fall of Vicksburg became known, and the great river was once more open from St. Louis to the sea.

In the north the victory of Gettysburg was won on the same day on which Vicksburg surrendered. A load of anxiety was lifted from the minds of the President and his ministers; the North took heart again, and resolved to continue the war with energy, in the hope of soon bringing it to a triumphant issue. The great and decisive event bringing about this change was the fall of Vicksburg, and the merit of that important success was due to Grant.

He had been successful, and in his success he still retained his freedom from "bounce" and from personal vanity; his steadfast concern for the public good; his moderation. Let us hear his account of being under fire during a fruitless attack by Admiral Porter's gunboats on the batteries of Grand Gulf:

"I occupied a tug, from which I could see the effect of the battle on both sides, within range of the enemy's guns; *but a small tug, without armament, was not calculated to attract the fire of batteries while they were being assailed themselves."*

He has to mention a risk incurred by himself; but mentioning it, he is at pains to minimise it.

When he assumed command in person at Young's Point, General McClernand, from whom the command now passed to Grant, his senior and superior, showed temper and remonstrated:

"His correspondence with me on the subject was more in the nature of a reprimand than a protest. It was highly insubordinate, *but I overlooked it, as I believed, for the good of the service.* General McClernand was a member of Congress when the Secession War broke out; he belonged to that party which furnished all the opposition there was to a vigorous prosecution of the war for saving the Union; but there was no delay in his declaring himself for the Union at all hazards, and there was no uncertain sound in his declaration of where he stood in the contest before the country."

To such a man Grant wished to be forbearing when he could say to himself that, after all, it was only his own dignity which was concerned. But later, when an irregularity of the same General was injurious to good feeling and unity in the army, Grant was prompt and severe:

"I received a letter from General Sherman, and one from General McPherson, saying that their respective commands had complained to them of a fulsome congratulatory order published by General McClernand to the 13th Corps, which did great injustice to the other troops engaged in the campaign. This order had been sent north and published, and now papers containing it had reached our camps. The order had not been heard of by me; I at once wrote to McClernand, directing him to send me a copy of this order. He did so, and I at once relieved him from the command of the 13th Army Corps. The publication of his order in the press was in violation of War Department orders, and also of mine."

The newspaper press is apt to appear to an American, even more than to an Englishman, as part of the order of nature, and contending with it seems like contending with destiny. Grant had governing instincts. "I always admired the South, as bad as I thought their cause, for the boldness with which they silenced all opposition and all croaking by press or by individuals within their control." His instincts would have led him to follow this example. But since he could do nothing against the newspaper nuisance, and was himself the chief sufferer by it, he bore it with his native philosophy:

"Visitors to the camps went home with dismal stories. Northern papers came back to the soldiers with these stories exaggerated. Because I would not divulge my ultimate plans to visitors, they pronounced me idle, incompetent, and unfit to command men in an emergency, and clamoured for my removal. They were not to be satisfied, many of them, with my simple removal, but named who my successor should be. I took no steps to answer these complaints, but continued to do my duty, as I understood it, to the best of my ability."

Surely the Duke of Wellington would have read these *Memoirs* with pleasure. He might himself have issued, too, this order respecting behaviour towards prisoners: "Instruct the commands to be quiet and orderly as these prisoners pass, and to make no offensive remark." And this other, respecting behaviour in a conquered enemy's country: "Impress upon the men the importance of going through the State in an orderly manner, abstaining from taking anything not absolutely necessary for their subsistence whilst travelling. They should try to create as favourable an impression as possible upon the people."

But what even at this stage of the war is very striking, and of good augury for the re-union which followed, is the absence, in general, of bitter hatred between the combatants. There is nothing of internecine, inextinguishable, irreconcilable enmity, or of the temper, acts, and words which beget this. Often we find the vanquished Southerner showing a good-humoured audacity, the victorious Northerner a good-humoured forbearance. Let us remember Carrier at Nantes, or Davoust at Hamburg, and then look at Grant's picture of himself and Sherman at Jackson, when their troops had just driven the enemy out of this capital of a "rebel" State, and were destroying the stores and war-materials there:

"Sherman and I went together into a manufactory which had not ceased work on account of the battle, nor for the entrance of Yankee troops. Our entrance did not seem to attract the attention of either the manager or the operatives, most of whom were girls. We looked on for a while to see the tent cloth which they were making roll out of the looms, with "C.S.A."* woven in each bolt. Finally I told Sherman I thought they had done work enough. The operatives were told they could leave, and take with them what cloth they could carry. In a few minutes the factory was in a blaze. The proprietor visited Washington, while I was President, to get his pay for this property, claiming that it was private."

The American girls coolly continuing to make the Confederate tents under the eye of the hostile generals, and the proprietor claiming afterwards to be paid by Congress for them as private property, are charming.

It was one of Grant's superstitions, he tells us, never to apply for a post, or to use personal or political influence for

*Confederate States Army.

obtaining it. He believed that if he had got it in this way he would have feared to undertake any plan of his own conception, for fear of involving his patrons in responsibility for his possible failure. If he were selected for a post, his responsibility ended, he said, with "his doing the best he knew how."

"Every one has his superstitions. One of mine is that in positions of great responsibility every one should do his duty to the best of his ability, where assigned by competent authority, without application or the use of influence to change his position. While at Cairo I had watched with very great interest the operations of the Army of the Potomac, looking upon that as the main field of the war. I had no idea, myself, of ever having any large command, nor did I suppose that I was equal to one; but I had the vanity to think that, as a cavalry officer, I might succeed very well in the command of a brigade. On one occasion, in talking about this to my staff officers, I said that I would give anything if I were commanding a brigade of cavalry in the Army of the Potomac, and I believed I could do some good. Captain Hellyer [Hillyer] suggested that I should make application to be transferred there to command the cavalry. I then told him that I would cut my right arm off first, and mentioned this superstition."

But now he was to be transferred, without any solicitation on his own part, to "the main field of the war." At first, however, he was appointed to the command of the "Military Division of the Mississippi," and after fighting a severe and successful battle at Chattanooga in November (1863), relieved that place and Knoxville, which the Confederates were threatening. President Lincoln, who had daily, almost hourly, been telegraphing to him to "remember Burnside," to "do something for Burnside," besieged in Knoxville, was overjoyed. "I wish," he wrote to Grant, "to tender you, and all under your command, my more than thanks, my profoundest gratitude, for the skill, courage and perseverance with which you and they, over so great difficulties, have effected this important object. God bless you all!" Congress voted him thanks and a gold medal for his achievements at Vicksburg and Chattanooga.

In the dead of the winter, with the thermometer below zero, he made an excursion into Kentucky, and had the pleasure of finding the people along his route, both in Tennessee and Kentucky, in general intensely loyal to the Union:

"They would collect in little places where we would stop of evenings, to see me. The people naturally expected to see the commanding general the oldest person in the party. I was then forty-one years of age, while my medical director was grey-haired, and probably twelve or more years my senior. The crowds would generally swarm around him, and thus give me an opportunity of quietly dismounting and getting into the house."

At the beginning of the next year, 1864, a Bill was passed through Congress for restoring the grade of Lieutenant-General in the army. Grant was nominated to that rank, and having been summoned to Washington he received his commission from the President on the 9th of March, in the presence of the Ministers. Before he came to Washington, he had meant to return to his command in the West even after being made lieutenant-general; but at Washington he saw reason to change his mind. The important struggle was now between the Army of the Potomac and Lee. From what he saw, Grant was convinced that in that struggle no one except himself, with the superior rank he now bore, could, probably, "resist the pressure that would be brought to bear upon him to desist from his own plans and pursue others." He obtained, therefore, the nomination of Sherman to succeed him in command of the Military Division of the Mississippi. On the 12th of March orders were published by the War Department, placing Grant in chief command of all the armies.

The position of General Meade, who was at that time in command of the Army of the Potomac, and who had won the important battle of Gettysburg in the previous summer, underwent a grave change through Grant's promotion. Both Meade and Grant behaved very well. Meade suggested to Grant that he might wish to have immediately under him Sherman, who had been serving with Grant in the West. He begged him not to hesitate in making the change if he thought it for the good of the service. The work in hand, he said, was of such vast importance, that the feelings and wishes of no one person should stand in the way of selecting the right men. He was willing himself to serve to the best of his ability wherever placed. Grant assured him that he had no thought of moving him, and in his *Memoirs*, after relating what had passed, he adds: "This incident gave me even a more favourable opinion of Meade than did his great victory at Gettysburg the July before. It is men who wait to be selected, and not those who seek, from whom we may always expect the most efficient service." He tried to make Meade's position as nearly as possible what it would have been had he himself been away in Washington or elsewhere; he gave all orders for the movements of the Army of the Potomac to Meade for execution, and to avoid the necessity of having to give direct orders himself, he established his headquarters close to Meade's whenever he could. Meade's position, however, was undoubtedly a somewhat embarrassing one; but its embarrassment was not increased by soreness on his part, or by want of delicacy on Grant's.

In the West, the great objects to be attained by Sherman were the defeat of Johnston and his army, and the occupation of Atlanta. These objects he accomplished, proceeding afterwards to execute his brilliant and famous march to Savannah and the sea, sweeping the whole State of Georgia. In the East, the opposing forces stood between the Federal and Confederate capitals, and substantially in the same relations to each other as when the war began three years before. President Lincoln told Grant, when he first saw him in private, that although he had never professed to know how campaigns should be conducted, and never wanted to interfere in them, yet "procrastination on the part of commanders, and the pressure from the people at the North and Congress, *which was always with him,* forced him into issuing his series of Military Orders. He did not know but they were all wrong, and did know that some of them were. What he wanted," he continued, "was a general who would take the responsibility and act; he would support him with all the power of the Government." He added that he did not even ask to know what Grant's plans were. But such is human nature, that the next moment he brought out a map of Virginia, showed Grant two streams running into the Potomac, and suggested a plan of his own for landing the army between the mouths of these streams, which would protect its flanks while it moved out. "I listened respectfully," says Grant, with dry humour, "but did not suggest that the same streams would protect Lee's flanks while he was shutting us up."

In Grant the President had certainly found a general who would take the responsibility, would act, and would keep his plans to himself. To beat Lee and get possession of his army, was the object. If Lee was beaten and his army captured, the fall of Richmond must necessarily follow.

If Richmond were taken by moving the army thither on transports up the James River, but meanwhile Lee's army were to remain whole and unimpaired, the end of the war was not brought any nearer. But the end of the war must be reached soon, or the North might grow weary of continuing the struggle. For three years the war had raged, with immense losses on either side, and no decisive consummation reached by either. If the South could succeed in prolonging an indecisive struggle year after year still, the North might probably grow tired of the contest, and agree to a separation. Persuaded of this Grant, at the beginning of May 1864, crossed the Rapidan with the Army of the Potomac, and commenced the forty-three days' Campaign of the Wilderness.

The Wilderness is a tract north of Richmond, between the Rapidan and the James River, much cut up with streams and morasses, full of broken ground, densely clothed with wood, and thinly inhabited. The principal streams between the Rapidan and the James River are the branches of the Anna, uniting in the Pamunkey, and the Chickahominy. The country was favourable for defence, and Lee was a general to make the most of its advantages. Grant was in an enemy's country, but, moving by his left flank, was in connection with the sea, of which the Northerners were masters, and was abundantly supplied with everything. Of artillery, in particular, he had so much that he was embarrassed by it, and had to send some of it away. Overwhelmingly superior in numbers and resources, he pressed steadily forward, failing and repulsed sometimes, but coolly persevering. This campaign, of which the stages are the battles of Chancellorsville,[7]

7. Grant's army passed through Chancellorsville during the Wilderness Campaign, but the battle of Chancellorsville had been fought the previous year.

Spottsylvania, North Anna and Cold Harbour, was watched at the time in Europe with keen attention, and is much better known than the operations in the West. I shall not attempt any account of it; for its severity let the losses of Grant's successful army speak. When he crossed the Rapidan the Army of the Potomac numbered 115,000 men; during the forty-three days' campaign reinforcements were received amounting to 40,000 men more. When the army crossed the James River, it was 116,000 strong, almost exactly the same strength as at the beginning of the campaign. Thirty-nine thousand men had been lost in forty-three days.

A yet greater loss must have been incurred had Grant attacked Lee's lines in front of Richmond; and therefore, crossing the James River, he invested, after failing to carry it by assault, Petersburg, the enemy's important stronghold south of Richmond. Winter came and passed. Lee's army was safe in its lines, and Richmond had not yet fallen; but the Confederates' resources were failing, their foes gathering, and the end came visibly near. After sweeping Georgia and taking Savannah in December, Sherman turned north and swept the Carolinas, ready to join with Grant in moving upon Lee in the spring. Sheridan made himself master of the Shenandoah Valley, and closed to the Confederates that great source of supply. Finally Grant, resuming operations in March 1865, possessed himself of the outer works of Petersburg, and of the railroad by which the place was supplied from the south-west, and on the 3rd of April Petersburg was evacuated. Then Grant proceeded to possess himself of the railroad by which Lee's army and Richmond itself now drew their supplies. Lee had already informed his government that he could hold out no longer. The Confederate President was at church when the despatch arrived, the congregation were told that there would be no evening service, and the authorities abandoned Richmond that afternoon. In the field there was some sharp fighting for a day or two still; but Lee's army was crumbling away, and on the 9th of April he wrote to Grant, requesting an interview with him for the purpose of surrendering his army. Grant was suffering from sick headache when the officer bearing Lee's note reached him, "but the instant I saw," he says, "the contents of the note, I was cured."

Then followed, in the afternoon of that same day, the famous interview at Appomattox Court House. Grant shall himself describe the meeting:

"When I had left camp that morning I had not expected so soon the result that was then taking place, and consequently was in rough garb. I was without a sword, as I usually was when on horseback in the field, and wore a soldier's blouse for a coat, with the shoulder-straps of my rank to indicate to the army who I was. When I went into the house I found General Lee. We greeted each other, and, after shaking hands, took our seats.

"What General Lee's feelings were I do not know. As he was a man of much dignity, with an impassible face, it was impossible to say whether he felt inwardly glad that the end had finally come, or felt sad over the result and was too manly to show it. Whatever his feelings, they were entirely concealed from my observation; but my own feelings, which had been quite jubilant on the receipt of his letter, were sad and depressed. I felt like anything rather than rejoicing at the downfall of a foe who had fought so long and valiantly, and had suffered so much for a cause, though that cause was, I believe, one of the worst for which a people ever fought.

"General Lee was dressed in a full uniform which was entirely new, and was wearing a sword of considerable value, very likely the sword which had been presented by the State of Virginia. In my rough travelling suit, the uniform of a private with the straps of a lieutenant-general, I must have contrasted very strangely with a man so handsomely dressed, six feet high and of faultless form. But this was not a matter that I thought of until afterwards.

"We soon fell into a conversation about old army times. He remarked that he remembered me well in the old army (of Mexico); and I told him that as a matter of course I remembered *him* perfectly, but from the difference in our rank and years (there being about sixteen years' difference in our ages) I had thought it likely that I had not attracted his attention sufficiently to be remembered by him after such a long interval. Our conversation grew so pleasant that I almost forgot the object of our meeting. After the conversation had run on in this style for some time, General Lee called my attention to the object of our meeting, and said that he had asked for this interview for the purpose of getting from me the terms I proposed to give his army. I said that I meant merely that his army should lay down their arms, not to take them up again during the continuance of the war unless duly and properly exchanged."

Lee acquiesced, and Grant, who throughout the interview seems to have behaved with true delicacy and kindness, proceeded to write out the terms of surrender. It occurred to him, as he was writing, that it would be an unnecessary humiliation to the officers to call upon them to surrender their side-arms, and also that they would be glad to retain their private horses and effects, and accordingly he inserted in the terms that the surrender of arms and property was not to include the side-arms, horses and property of the officers. Lee remarked that this would have a happy effect on the army. Grant then said that most of the men in Lee's ranks were, he supposed, small farmers; that the country had been so raided by either army that it was doubtful whether they would be able to put in a crop to carry themselves and their families through the next winter without the aid of the horses they were then riding; that the United States did not want them, and he would therefore give instructions to let every man of the Confederate army, who claimed to own a horse or mule, take the animal to his home. Again Lee remarked that this would have a happy effect.

At half-past four Grant could telegraph to the Secretary of War at Washington: "General Lee surrendered the army of Northern Virginia this afternoon." As soon as the news of the surrender became known, Grant's army began to fire a salute of a hundred guns. Grant instantly stopped it.

The war was at an end. Johnston surrendered to Sherman in North Carolina. President Lincoln visited Richmond, which had been occupied by the Army of the Potomac the day after the Confederate Government abandoned it. The President on his return to Washington invited Grant, who also had now gone thither, to accompany him to the theatre on the evening of the 14th of April. Grant declined, because he was to go off that evening to visit his children who were at school in New Jersey; when he reached Philadelphia, he heard that the President and Mr. Seward had been assassinated. He immediately returned to Washington, to find the joy there turned to mourning. With this tragic event, and with the grand review in the following month of Meade's and Sherman's armies by the new President, Mr. Johnson, the *Memoirs* end.

Modest for himself, Grant is boastful, as Americans are apt to be, for his nation. He says with perfect truth that troops who have fought a few battles and won, and followed up their victories, improve upon what they were before to an extent that can hardly be counted by percentage; and that his troops and Sherman's which had gone through this training, were by the end of the war become very good and seasoned soldiers. But he is fond of adding, in what I must call the American vein, "*better than any European soldiers.*" And the reason assigned for this boast is in the American vein too: "Because they not only worked like a machine, but the machine thought. European armies know very little what they are fighting for, and care less." Is the German army a machine which does not think? Did the French revolutionary armies know very little what they were fighting for, and care less? Sainte-Beuve says charmingly that he "cannot bear to have it said that he is the *first* in anything; it is not a thing that can be admitted, and these ways of classing people give offence." German military men read Grant's boast, and are provoked into replying that the campaigns and battles of the American Civil War were mere struggles of militia; English military men say that Americans have been steady enough behind breastworks and entrenchments against regulars, but never in the open field. Why cannot the Americans, in speaking of their nation, take Sainte-Beuve's happy and wise caution?

The point is worth insisting on, because to be always seeking to institute comparisons, and comparisons to the advantage of their own country, is with so many Americans a *tic*, a mania, which every one notices in them, and which sometimes drives their friends half to despair. Recent greatness is always apt to be sensitive and self-assertive; let us remember Dr. Hermann Grimm on Goethe. German literature, as a power, does not begin before Lessing; if Germany had possessed a great literature for six centuries, with names in it like Dante, Montaigne, Shakespeare, probably Dr. Hermann Grimm would not have thought it necessary to call Goethe the greatest poet that has ever lived. But the Americans in the rage for comparison-making beat the world. Whatever excellence is mentioned, America must, if possible, be brought in to balance or surpass it. That fine and delicate naturalist, Mr. Burroughs, mentions trout, and instantly he adds: "British trout, by the way, are not so beautiful as our own; they are less brilliantly marked and have much coarser scales, there is no gold or vermilion in their colouring." Here superiority is claimed; if there is not superiority there must be at least balance. Therefore in literature we have "the American Walter Scott," "the American Wordsworth"; nay, I see advertised *The Primer of American Literature*. Imagine the face of Philip or Alexander at hearing of a Primer of Macedonian Literature! Are we to have a Primer of Canadian Literature too, and a Primer of Australian? We are all contributories to one great literature—English Literature. The contribution of Scotland to this literature is far more serious and important than that of America has yet had time to be; yet a "Primer of Scotch Literature" would be an absurdity. And these things are not only absurd; they are also retarding.

My opinion on any military subject is of course worth very little, but I should have thought that in what Napier calls "strength and majesty" as a fighter, the American soldier, if we are to institute these comparisons, had his superiors; though as brave as any one, he is too ingenious, too mental, to be the perfection of a fighting animal. Where the Yankee soldier has an unrivalled advantage is in his versatility and ingenuity; dexterous, willing, suggestive, he can turn his hand to anything, and is of twenty trades at the same time with that of soldier. Grant's *Memoirs* are full of proofs of this faculty, which might perhaps be of no great use in a campaign in the Low Countries, but was invaluable in such campaigns as those which Grant and Sherman conducted in America. When the batteries at Vicksburg were to be run with hired river steamers, there were naturally but very few masters or crews who were willing to accompany their vessels on this service of danger. Volunteers were therefore called for from the army, men who had had any experience in river navigation. "Captains, pilots, mates, engineers, and deckhands, enough presented themselves," says Grant, "to take five times the number of vessels we were moving." The resource and rapidity shown by the troops in the repair of railroads wrecked by the enemy were marvellous. In Sherman's Atlanta campaign, the Confederate cavalry lurking in his rear to burn bridges and obstruct his communications had become so disgusted at hearing trains go whistling by, within a few hours after a bridge had been burned, that they proposed to try blowing up some of the tunnels. One of them said on this: "No use, boys; old Sherman carries duplicate tunnels with him, and will replace them as fast as you can blow them up; better save your powder!"

But a leader to use these capable and intelligent forces, to use all the vast resources of the North, was needed, a leader wise, cool, firm, bold, persevering, and at the same time, as Cardinal Mazarin says, *heureux*; and such a leader the United States found in General Grant.

He concludes his *Memoirs* by some advice to his own country and some remarks on ours. The United States, he says, are going on as if in the greatest security, "when they have not the power to resist an invasion by the fleets of fourth-rate European Powers for a time until we could prepare for them." The United States "should have a good navy, and our sea-coast defences should be put in the finest possible condition. Neither of these cost much when it is considered where the money goes and what we get in return."

The tone and temper of his remarks on England, and on her behaviour during the war, are in honourable contrast with the angry acrimony shown by many who should have known better. He regretted, he said, the exasperation. "The hostility of England to the United States, during our rebellion, was not so much real as it was apparent. It was the hostility of the leaders of one political party. England and the United States are natural allies, and should be the best of friends."

The *Memoirs* stop, as I have said, in 1865, and do not embrace Grant's Presidency, his journey to Europe, his financial disaster, his painful illness and death. As to his financial disaster, I will repeat what one of Grant's best friends, a man of great business faculty and of great fortune, remarked to me. I had been saying, what one says so easily, that it was a pity Grant had suffered himself to be drawn in by speculators. "Yes," answered his friend, "it was a pity. But see how it happened, and put yourself in Grant's place. Like Grant, you may have a son to whom you are partial, and like Grant, you have no knowledge of business. Had you been, like Grant, in a position to make it worth while for a leader in business and finance to come to you, saying that your son had a quite exceptional talent for these matters, that it was a thousand pities his talent should be thrown away, 'give him to me and I will make a man of him,' would you not have been flattered in your parental pride, would you not have yielded? This is what happened to Grant, and all his financial misfortunes flowed from hence." I listened, and could not deny that most probably I should have been flattered to my ruin, as Grant was.

Grant's *Memoirs* are a mine of interesting things; I have but scratched the surface and presented a few samples. When I began, I did not know that the book had been reprinted in England; I find that it has,* and that its circulation here, though trifling indeed compared to that in America, has been larger than I supposed. But certainly the book has not been read here anything like so much as it deserves. It contains a gallery of portraits, characters of generals who served in the war, for which alone the book, if it contained nothing else, would be well worth reading. But after all, its great value is in the character which, quite simply and unconsciously, it draws of Grant himself. The Americans are too self-laudatory, too apt to force the tone and thereby, as Sainte-Beuve says, to give offence; the best way for them to make us forgive and forget this is to produce what is simple and sterling. Instead of Primers of American Literature, let them bring forth more Maxims of Poor Richard; instead of assurances that they are "the greatest nation upon earth," let them give us more Lees, Lincolns, Shermans, and Grants.

*By Messrs. Sampson Low, Marston & Co.

# A Rejoinder by Mark Twain

*Speech at the Annual Reunion of the Army and Navy Club
of Connecticut, April 27, 1887*

I WILL DETAIN you with only just a few words—just a
few thousand words; and then give place to a better
man—if he has been created. Lately a great and honored
author. Matthew Arnold, has been finding fault with
General Grant's English. That would be fair enough,
may be, if the examples of imperfect English averaged
more instances to the page in General Grant's book than
they do in Mr. Arnold's criticism upon the book—but they
don't. [*Laughter and applause.*] It would be fair enough,
may be, if such instances were commoner in General
Grant's book than they are in the works of the average
standard author—but they aren't. In truth, General
Grant's derelictions in the matter of grammar and con-
struction are not more frequent than are such derelictions
in the works of a majority of the professional authors of
our time and of all previous times—authors as exclusively
and pains-takingly trained to the literary trade as was
General Grant to the trade of war. [*Applause.*] This is not
a random statement: it is a fact, and easily demonstrable.
I have at home a book called "Modern English Literature,
its Blemishes and Defects," by Henry H. Breen, F. S. A.,
a countryman of Mr. Arnold. In it I find examples of bad
grammar and slovenly English from the pens of Sydney
Smith, Sheridan, Hallam, Whately, Carlyle, both Dis-
raelis, Allison, Junius, Blair, Macaulay, Shakespeare,
Milton, Gibbon, Southey, Bulwer, Cobbett, Dr. Samuel
Johnson, Trench, Lamb, Landor, Smollett, Walpole,
Walker (of the dictionary), Christopher North, Kirke

[ 55 ]

White, Mrs. Sigourney, Benjamin Franklin, Walter Scott, and Mr. Lindley Murray, who made the grammar. In Mr. Arnold's paper on General Grant's book we find a couple of grammatical crimes and more than several examples of very crude and slovenly English—enough of them to easily entitle him to a lofty place in that illustrious list of delinquents just named. The following passage, all by itself, ought to elect him: "Meade suggested to Grant that he might wish to have immediately under him Sherman, who had been serving with Grant in the west. *He* begged *him* not to hesitate if *he* thought it for the good of the service. Grant assured *him* that *he* had no thought of moving *him*, and in *his* Memoirs, after relating what had passed, *he* adds," etc.[1] To read that passage a couple of times would make a man dizzy, to read it four times would make him drunk. [*Great laughter.*] General Grant's grammar is as good as anybody's: but if this were not so, Mr. Breen would brush that inconsequential fact aside and hunt his great book for far higher game. Mr. Breen makes this discriminating remark: "To suppose that because a man is a poet or a historian, he must be correct in his grammar, is to suppose that an architect must be a joiner, or a physician a compounder of medicines." Mr. Breen's point is well taken. If you should climb the mighty Matterhorn to look out over the kingdoms of the earth, it might be a pleasant incident to find strawberries up there; but, great Scott, you don't climb the Matterhorn for Strawberries! [*Continued applause.*]

I don't think Mr. Arnold was quite wise; for he well knew that that Briton or American was never yet born who could safely assault another man's English: he knew as well as he knows anything, that the man never lived

1. The passage quoted does not appear in this form in the original article or the Boston reprint.

whose English was flawless. Can you believe that Mr.
Arnold was immodest enough to imagine himself an exception to this cast iron rule—the sole exception discover-
able within the three or four centuries during which the
English language proper has been in existence? No, Mr.
Arnold did not imagine that: he merely forgot that for a
moment he was moving into a glass house, and he had
hardly got fairly in before General Fry was shivering the
panes over his head. [*Laughter.*]

People may hunt out what microscopic motes they
please, but, after all, the fact remains and can not be dis-
lodged that General Grant's book is a great, (and in its
peculiar department) unique and unapproachable literary
masterpiece. In their line there is no higher literature than
those modest, simple "memoirs." Their *style* is at least
flawless, and no man can improve upon it; and great books
are weighed and measured by their style and matter, not
by the trimmings and shadings of their grammar. There
is that about the sun which makes us forget his spots: and
when we think of General Grant our pulses quicken and
his grammar vanishes: we only remember that this is the
simple soldier who, all untaught of the silken phrase-
makers, linked words together with an art surpassing the
art of the schools, and put into them a something which
will still bring to American ears, as long as America shall
last, the roll of his vanished drums and the tread of his
marching hosts. [*Tumultuous applause.*] What do we care
for grammar when we think of the man that put together
that thunderous phrase, "Unconditional and immediate
surrender!" And those others: "I propose to move immediately upon your works!" "I propose to fight it out on
this line if it takes all summer!" [*Applause.*] Mr. Arnold
would doubtless claim that that last sentence is not strictly
grammatical; and yet nevertheless it did certainly wake

up this nation as a hundred million tons of A1, fourth proof, hard-boiled, hide-bound grammar from another mouth couldn't have done. And finally we have that gentler phrase: that one which shows you another true side of the man; shows that in his soldier heart there was room for other than gory war mottoes, and in his tongue the gift to fitly phrase them: "Let us have peace." [*Prolonged applause and cheers.*][2]

2. The text used here is taken from the *Hartford Courant*, April 28, 1887. Another version, somewhat shorter, appeared in the *New York World*, April 28, 1887, and is evidently the one used by James B. Fry in *Military Miscellanies* (New York, 1889), pp. 323–25. The *Courant* account apparently served as the basis for the version in the Paine edition of *Speeches of Mark Twain* (New York, 1923), pp. 135–37, but is both longer and more coherent than that in the Paine edition.

p 20. per Grant: Civil war
res. of Mex. war — South constantly
looking to expand own terr
& to impose slavery (own syst.)
drawing on name/res. of U.S.


p 44 most imp. task to
defeat Lee; capture of
Richmond involved.

p 49 G. modest for self, boastful
for country.

p 51 A. ref. to Amer. preoccup.
w/ comparisons. Like Trollope?

p 52 Mazzini — est-il sérieux!

Gnts. :  1) Didn't crit. Lincoln
         2) Didn't oppose Lincoln
            politically
         3) Didn't seek offices etc
         4) Knew self / self-controlled
            so could control others.
         5) Single minded re obj.